$\mathcal{B}$ONO

$\mathcal{B}$ONO

ROCK STAR & HUMANITARIAN

by Thom Winckelmann and Lynn Abushanab

Content Consultant:
Guy Capuzzo, PhD, Associate Professor
School of Music, University of North Carolina at Greensboro

ABDO
Publishing Company

CREDITS

Published by ABDO Publishing Company, 8000 West 78th Street, Edina, Minnesota 55439. Copyright © 2010 by Abdo Consulting Group, Inc. International copyrights reserved in all countries. No part of this book may be reproduced in any form without written permission from the publisher. The Essential Library™ is a trademark and logo of ABDO Publishing Company.

Printed in the United States.

 PRINTED ON RECYCLED PAPER

Editor: Nadia Higgins
Copy Editor: Patricia Stockland
Interior Design and Production: Emily Love
Cover Design: Emily Love

Library of Congress Cataloging-in-Publication Data
Winckelmann, Thom.
  Bono : rock star & humanitarian / by Thom Winckelmann & Lynn Abushanab.
      p. cm. — (Essential lives)
  Includes bibliographical references and index.
  ISBN 978-1-60453-698-0 (alk. paper)
  1. Bono, 1960-—Juvenile literature. 2. Rock musicians—Biography—Juvenile literature. I. Abushanab, Lynn. II. Title.

  ML3930.B592W56 2010
  782.42166092—dc22
  [B]   5671

                          2008055538

TABLE OF CONTENTS

In London, a huge crowd enjoys the Live Aid concert in July 1985.

LEAPS OF FAITH

In July 1985, Bono and U2 were presented with a rare opportunity. The rock band was to perform alongside some of the greatest musicians of the century, including Bob Dylan, David Bowie, and Mick Jagger. Their performance was to be televised live to a worldwide audience of 1.5 billion people. The event, called Live Aid, was to raise money for some of the poorest people on the planet—those starving in the African nation of Ethiopia.

The band had 15 minutes to play. Bono and the other members of U2— Larry Mullen (drums), Adam Clayton (bass), and The Edge (guitar)—agreed on a strict playlist. They did not want anything to go wrong.

When the band took the stage in London, things began as planned. They performed their hit "Sunday Bloody Sunday." Next up was "Bad," a song about drug addiction. But Bono did not want to play it the usual way. He started improvising, leading his band members through new territory.

Then, all of a sudden, Bono was overtaken by an urge—one that would lead him very far off the plan. For, down below, a fan was struggling in the crowd. The audience was several

"I thank God on a daily basis for my life in U2 because not only did this job put my talents to use, it put my insecurities and weaknesses to use. That's the miracle for me. So the emptiness you're feeling through absence or the desire for meaning and purpose in your life, all that ache, it suits a performer, because you're trying to fill the God-shaped hole with the crowd, your audience."[1]

—*Bono*

feet removed from the stage. Bono wanted to help her. What could he do?

A Leap Offstage

Bono leaped a full ten feet (3 m) off the stage. He argued with security staff to let him into the audience. For a full five minutes, he was lost in the crowd while his bandmates played the important gig without their lead singer. When Bono came back, he brought the stunned girl with him, and the two danced together onstage. Bono had wasted so much time, the band ended up skipping the third song on their playlist, their hit "Pride (In the Name of Love)." Bono noted later that the band was extremely upset with him for disrupting the plan to seek a publicity moment. Why did Bono do such a thing? He recalls:

> I was trying to find an image just to communicate how we all felt on that day. That was an overpowering day. It was a day that made tiny everybody that was in it, and the subject was so much bigger than anyone on the stage. I was not happy with just playing our songs and getting out of there.[2]

Bono had made a gut decision. It was the act of a man known for being an extreme performer, a stuntman, a person who looks to expand the boundary of each situation. It was an act of a man moved by the cause of Africa and also by the sight of a fan struggling in the crowd. And, like many of Bono's later decisions, though it seemed rash at first, it turned out to be inspired.

Bono's leap had captivated fans worldwide. As Edge later remarked, "There was something about the amount of effort he had to put into it to do it that somehow made it very powerful."[3] After Live Aid, U2 went from superstars to legends. Though more famous bands played that day, Bono and U2 stole the show.

Strong Words

In the mid-1980s, U2 was becoming known as a group that delivered rock with a message rather than superficial pop. The night before Live Aid, U2 issued the following statement. It shows a band willing not only to stand up for humanitarian causes but also to stand up to those in power.

U2 are involved in Live Aid because it's more than money, it's music—but it is also a demonstration to the politicians and the policy-makers that men, women and children will not walk by other men, women and children as they lie, bellies swollen, starving to death for the sake of a cup of grain and some water. For the price of Star Wars [a weapons program], the MX missile offensive-defensive budgets, the desert of Africa could be turned into fertile lands. The technology is with us. The technocrats are not. Are we part of a civilization that protects itself by investing in life—or investing in death?[4]

Bono in 1985

A Life-Changing Trip

Soon after Live Aid, Bono took another leap
of faith. He wanted to put substance behind his
symbolic actions at Live Aid. He took his first of
many trips to Africa. He and his wife, Ali Hewson,
were put in charge of an orphanage in Ethiopia for

six weeks. There, Bono says, "My life changed. . . . I saw things you shouldn't ever see."[5] He said:

> *You'd wake up in the morning, and the mist would be lifting. You'd walk out of your tent, and you'd count bodies of dead and abandoned children. Or worse, the father of a child would walk up to you and try to give you his living child and say, 'You take it, because if this is your child, it won't die.'*[6]

Bono believed that deep injustice caused such extreme poverty. He blamed Africa's crushing debt to rich nations and lack of trade as two major forces. He also recognized the devastating effects of racism. The world would never sit idly by if such misery were taking place in France or England. Why was the world letting Africa down?

Compelled by his Christian beliefs that the poorest of the poor are closest to God, Bono took on

Why Africa?

Why is Bono so passionate about Africa? Because according to him, "sixty-five hundred Africans are dying every day of a preventable, treatable disease [AIDS]. And it's not a priority for the West: two 9/11s a day, eighteen jumbo jets of fathers, mothers, families falling out of the sky. No tears, no letters of condolence, no fifty-one-gun salutes. Why? Because we don't put the same value on African life as we put on a European or an American life. God will not let us get away with this."[7]

Africa as *his* cause. Little did he know that his work on behalf of Africa would take him to the highest offices of power, including those of presidents and the pope. It would earn him some of the world's most prestigious humanitarian awards.

Who Is Bono?

Many labels could describe Bono. He is an Irish rock star, a singer, and U2's main songwriter. Since U2 began in 1976, the band has sold more than 145 million records and won 22 Grammy awards.

Bono is a risk-taker. He has changed his image and U2's sound many times over the decades. He has walked into failure. As Bono's biographer and friend Michka Assayas has noted, "With each new record [U2] made, the band thought it was committing commercial suicide. And each time, success came back with a vengeance."[8]

"[U2's manager] Paul McGuinness has said to me all my life, 'Look, the job of the artist is to point out problems and not try and solve them.' But I have always seen creativity in places where you're not supposed to find it, in commerce and in politics. The same lateral thinking that works in the studio where you're pulling a melody out of thin air, I try to make it work for me wherever I am. I want to live the creative life not just do creative things in my life. And I think I turned out to be pretty good at this stuff."[9]

—Bono

But as much as he seeks change, Bono is loyal. Few bands in the history of rock have lasted as long as U2. Also unusual is Bono's lasting marriage to Ali Hewson, whom he started dating when he was 16.

Bono is a father of four. He is a Christian. At one point in his life, he was zealous in his beliefs. Today, while he does not regularly attend church services, his beliefs are at the core of everything he does.

Bono is a humanitarian who has founded several organizations in the fight against extreme poverty, particularly in Africa. He is a diplomat who wears T-shirts and sunglasses. Bono is a businessman with a conscience.

Who is Bono? Perhaps he answers the question best himself:

> *I'm a scribbling, cigar-smoking, wine-drinking, Bible-reading band man. A show-off . . . who loves to paint pictures*

Tightrope Walker

Bono recounted a conversation he had with Elvis Costello, a fellow musician:

"[Costello] said to me, 'I'm ambivalent about U2, I love it and I hate it.' He said, 'You walk this tightrope that none of your contemporaries will walk—they're afraid to walk it—and when you stay on I bow my head, but you fall off it so many times.' There was no answer to that. We do fall off, a lot, and on stage I'll try for something and it won't work . . . but it might work and that's the point—it *might* work."[10]

of what I can't see. A husband, father, friend of the poor and sometimes the rich. An activist traveling salesman of ideas. Chess player, part-time rock star, opera singer, in the loudest folk group in the world.[11] ⌐

Bono jokes around with Mtho Moya, a boy from an African orphanage, in 2007. Mtho is wearing Bono's sunglasses.

Downtown Dublin, the city of Bono's childhood, in 1969

DUBLIN CHILDHOOD

Bono was born Paul David Hewson on May 10, 1960, in Dublin, Ireland. "I was a freckle-faced kid who was difficult to tie down from the very beginning, a messer full of life, noisy, maybe a little too much testosterone," Bono says.[1]

"Sitting on the Fence"

Bono's father, Brendan Robert Hewson (known as Bobby), was a postal worker. Bono's mother, Iris Elizabeth Hewson, was working in an office when she met Bobby. Bono had one sibling, Norman, who was seven years older.

Bono jokingly describes his parents' marriage as almost criminal because his father was Catholic and his mother was Protestant. Those two religions have had a long, violent history in Ireland. In a mixed marriage, the nation's tradition was for the children to be brought up in the Catholic faith. But Bono's parents compromised. Bono's father attended services at the Catholic church, but Bono went to the Protestant church with his mother and brother. There, he found his first musical inspiration in the psalms and the hymns. He also acquired a deep Christian faith that would sustain him—in some form—throughout his life. But perhaps the most lasting impact of his childhood church experience was the impression made by his parents, whose extraordinary cooperation showed that peace was possible between two opposite groups. Bono would grow up to be a peacemaker, deeply offended by bigotry of any sort.

As an adult, Bono once said, "I always felt like I was sitting on the fence."[2] The fence separated his Protestant and Catholic sides. It also straddled the working-class and middle-class worlds of Dublin. While his neighborhood was lower middle-class, his family was relatively well-to-do. They owned a three-bedroom house with a nice backyard and were one of the few families who owned a car. At the same time, the neighborhood was a rough one. Street fights were an everyday occurrence. As he grew older, Bono learned well how to defend himself.

EARLY MEMORIES

Bono says that he has few memories from his childhood, but his first day of school stands out. Bono recalls:

> *A boy came up to my new best mate . . . and bit his ear, and I took that kid's head and banged it on some iron railings. . . . [T]hat is the sort of thing I remember. The little pieces that I can put back together are, if not violent, then aggressive.*[3]

On the other hand, Iris remembered a sweet, peaceful side of her son. At three, Bono was playing with bees in the backyard. Completely unaware of any danger, he picked up the bees. In his three-year-old way, he talked and sang to them. Then he put them back unharmed.

As a child, Bono's life was filled with music—opera music. Bobby was a talented amateur opera singer. He liked to blast opera while "conducting" with knitting needles. And yet, Bobby did anything but encourage his youngest son's interest in music. Bobby had given up his own artistic ambitions at 14, when he left school to begin a "practical" career as a civil servant. He wanted his son to do the same.

Bono's early interest in music showed in his love for his grandmother's piano. He would sit underneath that piano, listening to the sounds reverberate. He experimented with the keys. And yet, Bono's father refused to let him take piano lessons. Later, after Bono's grandmother died, the family sold the piano. Bono was devastated.

"My father's advice to me, without ever speaking it, was: 'Don't dream! To dream is to be disappointed.'"[4] And yet Bobby Hewson's unspoken advice backfired. After the incident with the piano, Bono's determination to succeed was even greater.

Cry Baby

According to Bono, he cried for hours on end as a baby. It was so bad, in fact, that his father would wait until the baby had gone to bed before coming home from work. At age three, Bono was taken to the hospital, where he was diagnosed with an unusual heartbeat. Bono still has an "eccentric" heart, though it presents no ill effects to his health.

For him, to pursue his dreams was the ultimate rebellion.

Early Ambitions

Bono was driven by an intellectual curiosity as well as a passion for wandering. He would intensely take on a subject that fascinated him, only to move on to the next. For example, he once read a book about chess and started learning the game with great passion. By 12, he rose to tournament level. But by the next year, he was into painting, then acting.

Bobby Hewson

Bono described his father as "a very charming, very amusing, very likable man, but he was deeply cynical about the world and the characters in it: affection for the few, a sort of scant praise on them. . . . I got to make peace with him, but never really to become his friend."[5]

A few years after U2 had become a major success, Hewson attended a U2 concert in Texas. When Bono introduced his father from stage in front of thousands of audience members, Hewson just shook his fist. After the concert, Bono's father came up to him with watering eyes. "This is the moment I've waited for all my life," Bono recalled. "My father was going to tell me he loves me. And he walked up, he put his hand out, a little shaky, a little unsteady ... and he said, 'Son . . . you're very professional!'"[6] In his reserved way, Hewson had let Bono know, finally, that he was proud of him.

Over the remaining years of Hewson's life, the two would enjoy a closer relationship. As Hewson lay dying of cancer, Bono flew home from gigs to sit by his bedside. Bono read to him the works of Shakespeare, Hewson's favorite writer. At his father's funeral in 2001, Bono sang "Sometimes You Can't Make It On Your Own," a song he wrote for him.

As he became a teenager, girls were another ambition, and Bono's attentions were almost always generously returned. Academically, he excelled in history, art, and drama.

He also developed an interest in music. Though he did not own any records of his own, he listened to his brother's cassette tapes of rock legends such as the Who and Jimi Hendrix. He developed a passion for John Lennon and David Bowie in particular. On warm days, Bono rode his bike to school so that he could stop off at record stores on the way home and listen to new releases.

Listening to music was one thing, though, and playing it was another. Bono's brother Norman started to teach Bono how to play the guitar. However, the lessons stopped after just three chords. Bono did not have the patience to practice.

MOUNT TEMPLE HIGH SCHOOL

In 1971, when Bono was 11, his parents enrolled him at a strictly run Protestant school called St. Patrick's. Bored and restless, Bono spent most school days walking the streets of Dublin. When he did show up at school, the day rarely went well. He held a particular hatred for his Spanish teacher.

One day he followed her to a city park, where she sat on a bench to eat her lunch. From behind a bush, Bono threw dog feces at her. That was the last straw. He was quickly expelled.

What happened next was probably one of the most fortunate events in Bono's life. He started at Mount Temple High School, Dublin's only nondenominational school, which meant both Protestants and Catholics could attend. It also was unique in that boys and girls sat in class together, and no uniforms were required. To get there and back, Bono had to ride his bike seven miles (11 km) a day, but he did not mind. He was free to be himself.

Little did Bono know how important his Mount Temple experience would prove to be. For here, he would meet the future members of U2—as well as his future wife. In the meantime, though, he had a tragedy to undergo. It was to be the defining event of his youth.

As a youth, Bono shared a stormy relationship with his father, though they later reconciled. Here, Bono carries his father's coffin in 2001.

The international sensation that was to be U2 began in 1976.

TROUBLED TEEN

*I*n 1974, Bono's maternal grandfather died. At the funeral, Bono watched his mother collapse. Doctors soon discovered that she had suffered a brain hemorrhage. Bono's mother died four days later, on September 10. Bono was just 14.

After Iris

"The death of my mother really affected my confidence," Bono remembers.

I would go back to my house after school, but it wasn't a home. She was gone. Our mother was gone, the beautiful Iris. . . . I felt abandoned, afraid. I guess fear converts to anger pretty quickly. It's still with me.[1]

For the next two years, Bono spun out of control. He attacked a teacher. He picked fights with his older brother Norman. Two entire weeks from this period in Bono's life are completely lost—he was so grief-stricken that he cannot remember anything from them.

Bono believed he was going crazy. He also experienced a crisis of faith. How could God let this happen? What did it mean? What did his life mean? Why did people die? These questions—as bleak as they were—inspired something inside the teenage boy. "I think my whole creative life goes back to when my world collapsed, age fourteen," Bono says. "The first thing I started writing about was death."[2] Indeed, Bono's life and U2's music would be informed by a deep sense of injustice that began during this period.

It was not until 1976 that Bono's life really started
to turn around. In that year, two events happened
that, Bono says, literally saved his life. First, he
started dating Alison Stewart, known as Ali, who
would become his wife. Soon after, the band that was
to become U2 met in Larry Mullen's kitchen.

A Teenage Spat

Inspired by the punk rock
movement of the time,
Bono was one of the first
students at Mount Tem-
ple to dress like a punk
rocker. But one time he
went overboard for his
girlfriend Ali. He showed
up at school with a chain
running from his earring
to his cheek. It looked like
he had pierced his cheek,
but had not really done
so. Ali was horrified—
and she let her boyfriend
know it.

Ali

Ali was born in Dublin in 1961.
Bono had met the dark-haired beauty
on his first day at Mount Temple. He
was immediately stricken, especially
by the air of confidence she exuded.
"There was something so still about
her, and to a person who is not still,
it was the most attractive thing in the
world," Bono recalls.[3]

And yet, Ali was not initially
stricken by Bono. She rebuffed
his first attempts to flirt with her.
Though Bono moved on to date
several other girls, Ali never left
his mind. At last, in 1976, the two
began a passionate and somewhat
stormy teenage romance. But it was

Bono and his wife, Ali Hewson, met as teenagers.

a romance that would continue to mature. Ali kept
Bono grounded in the midst of his turbulent teens—
and continues to do so today.

A Band Begins

U2 began with drummer Larry Mullen's hand-
written notice for musicians on a bulletin board at
Mount Temple. On September 25, 1976, the four

future members of U2, as well as some others, met in the Mullens' kitchen.

"We were all pretty crap," Edge remembers.[4] That included Bono, who arrived with a vague ambition to be a guitarist, though he knew only three chords. Fortunately, his other talents became obvious right away. Larry remembers:

> *Bono arrived, and he meant to play the guitar, but he couldn't play very well, so he started to sing. He couldn't do that either. But he was such a charismatic character that he was in the band anyway, as soon as he arrived. I was in charge for the first five minutes, but as soon as Bono got there, I was out of a job.[5]*

The band, called Feedback, began regular rehearsals at school and in the shed of Edge's family home. The group started by doing covers, performing other famous songs of

"We were four people before we were four musicians. When we started out we couldn't play any instruments. We built the band around the drum kit but when we were on stage we were a shambles. It was like every night we'd want to break up, but then every morning we'd wake up and want to start again."[6]

—*Bono on U2's early days*

the day. One of their first concerts was a talent show at Mount Temple. They lost, but they received a lot of applause. The audience recognized a creative spark, a showmanship, an honesty, and a drive that would one day propel the group into superstardom.

But first, they had to start writing their own songs. Bono's mind was already full of poetry. How would he channel it into songs?

Luckily for him, the whole idea of rock and roll had been recently turned on its head by the punk rock movement. New punk bands, including the Ramones and the Sex Pistols, introduced a

The Other Three Teenagers

• Drummer Larry Mullen was just 15 when he posted the fateful notice on the bulletin board. His family had recently bought him a used drum kit. He realized that his practice could only go so far by himself. He needed other musicians to play with. Like Bono, Mullen would lose his mother when he was a teenager, an event that would bring the two band members close together.

• Known today as The Edge, Dave Evans is U2's guitarist. The Edge got his first guitar at age eight, and he was obsessed with it. He was the only member who could play well in U2's early days. Ironically, he was perhaps the least enthusiastic. Shy by nature, he planned on becoming a doctor but was willing to give the band a try.

• Adam Clayton was regarded as the wild one, the chain-smoking rebel who liked to party. Clayton's bad behavior at school, including once running naked down the halls, got him expelled from Mount Temple in 1978. In 1976, bass player Clayton was the only teenager who had actually been in a band before. Though his image was impressive, it turned out that he actually could not play very well.

"do-it-yourself" attitude to music. The technical virtuosity of "progressive rock" as well as disco's dance beat were cast aside in favor of the raw energy of punk music. Punk music made an opening for Bono, and while his music imitated the edginess and energy of the sound, it also veered away. Punk music was nihilistic, opposed to the idea that life was meaningful. That idea did not suit Bono at all.

Bruce Springsteen's album *Born to Run* had just come out the previous year, and Bono was completely taken with the power and feeling of Springsteen's lyrics. Springsteen was a storyteller, and Bono admired the music's integrity and lack of ego.

So, while working part-time at a gas station, Bono started writing music. His work combined punk's attitude with soulfulness—an unusual combination that was to become a trademark of U2.

New Names

Feedback's next name was the Hype, picked mostly because the band members thought it sounded cool. As friendships cemented, the group's sound became harder and rockier.

Around this time, Bono was also experiencing a name change. He was now part of a loose group of friends known as the Lypton Village. The Village traipsed through Dublin in outrageous costumes, staying out late, and performing theatrical pranks. As Bono recalls, the Village was

> *an imaginary place, somewhere we developed in our imaginations to give us an alternative lifestyle as kids. We grew up studying people on street corners. We laughed at the way they talked and at the expressions they made. We mocked the adult world and agreed we would never grow up because all we saw was silliness.*[7]

The Village was a way for Bono to escape the violence and drinking of his rough neighborhood. It was also a chance to create a new identity. Village members invented their own language, and they were each given new names. Bono, who had been known by his birth name of Paul to that point, became Bono Vox, after the name of a hearing-aid store. But the name fit, as *Bono Vox* loosely translates to "good voice" in Latin.

Eventually, Bono Vox was shortened to just Bono. And The Hype was shortened, too. In early 1978, the group changed its name for a third and final time. The new name was a compromise, not particularly promoted by any of the members.

Bobby and the Village

Needless to say, Bono's father was not pleased with his son's membership in the Village. One night, Gavin Friday, another member of the group, showed up at the Hewson house wearing a full-length dress. Hewson was not amused by the stunt, telling Bono's friend that this was the last time he would be permitted into the house. As for the name "Bono," Hewson refused to use it. "Your mother christened you Paul, and Paul you are going to remain," he said.[8]

But it had a few things going for it. It was the name of an American spy plane, which lent an aura of coolness. It was different from other band names. It was open-ended, so fans could bring their own meaning to the name. Sometime after the name was chosen, Bono realized it was perhaps *too* open-ended. But it was too late. U2 the band—and the name—was here to stay.

Bono (front center) *and his fellow bandmates in 1979*

In 1980, U2 band members, from left to right, are Adam Clayton, Larry Mullen, Bono, and The Edge.

RISE TO FAME

More and more, the band played professional gigs at pubs and local clubs. Their fame was growing, but the work was not easy. Some of the clubs were in rough areas of Dublin. On more than one occasion, the audience threw glass bottles at the musicians. After one so-so performance, the band was pelted with lit cigarettes. At times, it took all of Bono's inner strength to resist retaliating with violence. After each of these gigs, Bono and the others did a "post-mortem," to analyze the strengths and weaknesses of their performance. They were deeply critical of themselves.

Irish Rock Stars

Then, in the Irish city of Limerick, the band got a big break. It won a talent contest and a sizeable cash prize. The group also earned a deal to cut a three-song extended play (EP) record. U2 became Irish rock stars.

The teenagers had charisma, talent, and improved musical abilities. But they did not have the skills and the savvy to handle the business side of things. They needed a manager. Ten years older than Bono, Paul McGuinness was a local film producer who had successfully promoted one other rock band. U2 pursued McGuinness, who was reluctant to take them on. But the band kept nagging him until he agreed to at least watch them perform. At the performance, McGuinness was immediately taken by

Bono and U2. By May 1978, McGuinness was U2's manager and has been so ever since.

Paul McGuinness

All of U2's members say that their band manager, Paul McGuinness, has been key to their success. Bono says, "More than anyone in my life, he is a person who believed in me and gave me the confidence to realize my potential as an artist. He has an enormous and sharp intellect, and mine was very unschooled and haphazard."[1]

Paul McGuinness's talents seem to complement Bono's in another way. McGuinness was never interested in being a musician himself. However, he has always been a huge music fan. As a band manager, he enjoyed the combination of creativity, music, and cultural impacts.

In 1978, McGuinness had been looking for an Irish band that he could take to the top. He had been managing another band, called Spud, which was not doing very well. However, the experience taught him what to look for in a band and how to handle business dealings.

He first heard U2's music when Adam Clayton, who had been calling him repeatedly, showed up at his house with a demo tape. McGuinness did not even own a tape recorder, so they played the tape in his answering machine. After that, he agreed to go see U2 live. What struck him most about U2's performance was Bono's commanding stage presence. McGuinness was one of the first to recognize what was to become a music phenomenon.

THE NEXT STEP

In September 1979, U2 put out its EP, entitled *U2:3*. The record topped the charts in Ireland. Now the band set its sights on international audiences, and the next natural step was a tour of Britain.

In December, U2 arrived at London's Hope & Anchor Pub. The Irish rock stars performed in front of just nine people. Though later gigs managed

to attract double-digit sized crowds, that early gig
set the tone of the British tour. Many clubs did
not even bother to get the band's name right. Even
when hailed as V2 or UR, however, the band played
with enthusiasm and heart. Bono was able to keep
it all in perspective—though at the time his attitude
could certainly have been interpreted as arrogance
or worse. "I want people in London to see and hear
the band," he said in an interview. "I want to replace
the bands in the charts now, because I think we're
better."[2]

Boy

After the tour, U2 returned to Dublin. Many
years later, even after the band had reached
superstardom, the city of Bono's childhood
would always be his home base. Bono has said that
Dubliners are naturally suspicious of the glamour
and distortions of show business. The city inspires
Bono, and it offers him perspective.

And, after the dismal British tour, Dublin
offered just what the band needed in early 1980. Bill
Stewart of Island Records, a major music label, came
to see the group perform. He later described his
experience:

One bitterly cold night in February 1980, a shivering talent-spotter found himself in Dublin on what was beginning to look like another wild goose chase. . . . Suddenly in a burst of white light four slight figures pounced on stage, picked up their instruments as if they were soldiers seizing weapons and tore into their first song with a deafening roar. It was electrifying. It was the first night I saw U2.[3]

Island Records offered U2 an attractive deal, but the band did not jump at it. Over the years, U2 would earn a reputation for being fiercely protective of its creative freedom. So, while Island Records promised money beyond the scope of what they had ever had, the band members insisted on something unheard-of in music contracts. Island records would accept U2's next four albums once they were completely finished. That way, the music would be untouched by suggestions or interference from music-industry professionals.

The deal was signed, and in October 1980, U2 released its first full-length album. *Boy* was a brash album, layered with loud guitars and Bono's yelping voice. Songs, including the hit "I Will Follow," addressed themes of childhood and adolescence. They described exuberance, faith, and disappointment. *Boy* introduced U2 as an original band not content with the bubblegum pop of the day. And though the album did not sell particularly well, it was generally well reviewed. U2's "highly original sound can perhaps be best described as pop music with brains," wrote James Henke of *Rolling Stone.*[4]

ON TO AMERICA

The release of *Boy* marked the beginning of another aspect of Bono's life—almost constant travel. In the fall of 1980, the band headed overseas for its first of many U.S. tours. On a November night in Boston, U2 got a taste of what the United States had in store. Though it was opening for another band, U2 was called back for an encore. With the crowd still screaming, the band headed to its dressing room—only to be brought back onstage for yet another encore.

"I Will Follow"

Boy's biggest single was "I Will Follow," a song Bono wrote about unconditional love between a mother and a child. It is written from the point of view of the mother, saying, "Walk away, walk away . . . I will follow." At the same time, the tender lyrics are set against a hard, pounding beat. Bono describes it as "the sound of a nail being hammered into your frontal lobe," explaining that it came out of a screaming argument during rehearsal.[5]

Bono would soon say to a *Rolling Stone* reporter:

I don't mean to sound arrogant, but even at this stage, I do feel that we are meant to be one of the great groups. There's a certain spark, a certain chemistry, that was special about the Stones, the Who and the Beatles, and I think it's also special about U2.[6]

Bono performs in California in U2's early days.

Bono in 1981

Rock Star

The spring of 1981 was a stressful time for Bono. A grueling U.S. tour meant almost constant travel. At the same time, he was writing U2's second album. But perhaps most stressful, Bono started to deeply question his career.

Identity Crisis

By the early 1980s, Bono, Larry, Edge, and Ali had joined a Christian group called Shalom, a word that means "peace" in Hebrew. The group encouraged a deeply spiritual life, stripped of all vanity and ego. As U2's fame increased, members of Shalom started pressuring them to quit the band. Bono began to feel pulled in two opposite directions. On one hand, he was striving to be meek and humble. On the other hand, he was a rock star.

During 12-hour bus rides, Bono, Edge, and Larry would be in the back of the bus reading Bible passages, while Adam and Paul McGuinness sat in front. As the only band member not in Shalom, Adam began to feel more and more like an outsider in his own group. It began to look like U2 might not survive. With each gig, there was the unspoken question: would this be U2's last?

Bono's questions about his identity lasted for the next several years. In November 1981, Bono and Edge actually quit the band, telling McGuinness to cancel a tour they had

Bono on Shalom

How were Bono and his bandmates able to be so influenced by a radical Christian group? Shalom was, Bono says, "a community the like of which we'd never seen before. They were on the street, living like first-century Christians. They believed in miracles as a daily business, and they lived the life of faith. They were fascinating."[1]

scheduled. But McGuinness convinced them to at
least uphold their commitments. In the end, Bono
realized that he could serve God through his music.
Bono's songs might aspire to great ideals, but he does
not have to be the living emblem of those ideals. He
says:

> *The eighties were a prison of self-consciousness. . . . Now, I*
> *don't feel I have to prove myself to anyone. It's like: Are your*
> *songs any good? Is your band any good? That's it, mate. I*
> *can't live up to the songs. These songs are better than me.*
> *Don't fence me in as a good person, because I'm going to let*
> *you down. Hey, I'm complex. I'm an artist! I can be a jerk.*
> *I'm over it.* [2]

OCTOBER

Bono's music is deeply inspired by his personal
experience. It makes sense that the group's second
album, *October,* released October 1981, would be
deeply religious. Songs such as "Gloria," "Fire," and
"Is That All?" touch on the album's theme of the
journey of the spiritual life. The album alludes often
to the Bible and to Christ. Many people wondered if
U2 had become a Christian rock band. Some former
fans were turned off. But the album, which brought

mixed reviews, brought new fans as well. It sold better than *Boy.*

Bono says that he was not, or has never been, out to convert anybody. The album was "a kind of religious experience" for him.[3] He explains how it grew from the experience of the Shalom group. In his personal life, he had been willing to let go of U2—the thing he had always wanted more than anything else. That willingness to start over translated to the album. *October* was where U2 said:

> *We will go wherever we have to go. We will break all rules of hipness. We will be as raw emotionally as we have to be, in order to be honest.* [4]

"Two Hearts Beat As One"

The album was followed, in 1982, by another tour. U2 opened for big acts. They played at their largest venues yet and in cities they would not have seen on their own.

When they returned home that summer, they were exhausted and broke. Despite the distance between

"Gloria"

October was recorded under pressure. Much of the album was improvised at the studio, including "Gloria." Bono's band members were waiting for a song, but Bono could not think of what to write. So he started to write about that—about having nothing to say. The song "Gloria" was inspired by that struggle: "I try to stand up but I can't find my feet. I try to speak up but only in you [God] I'm complete. . . . Oh, Lord, loosen my lips."[5]

Bono's choice of Adam Clayton (left, in 1997) as his best man brought Bono closer to U2.

them, Bono and Ali had continued to grow close. On August 21, 1982, the two married at a modest service in Dublin. Bono was 22 years old.

Bono made a surprise choice for his best man. He chose Adam—the one U2 member who had not been caught up in Shalom. "I asked [Adam] because maybe I didn't feel as close with him as I did with the others," Bono would later say.[6] Through his marriage ceremony, Bono not only committed to Ali but, symbolically, he recommitted to U2 as well.

While honeymooning in the Bahamas, Bono wrote one of U2's few love songs—"Two Hearts Beat As One," a newly married man's tribute to his wife.

"Sunday Bloody Sunday"

Meanwhile, back in Ireland, Edge was working along a completely different theme. He started writing a song about the so-called Troubles in Northern Ireland. Since the 1960s, this area had been rocked by violence, stemming from deep divisions between its two main groups. The unionists were generally Protestants who

"Not a Rebel Song"

In "Sunday Bloody Sunday," Bono's passionate singing overlays a fierce, pounding beat. Bono sings about the futility of violence:

Broken bottles under children's feet/Bodies strewn across a dead-end street/But I won't heed the battle call/It puts my back up, my back up against the wall

He goes on to address the complicity of the audience, bystanders (including him) whose reality has been distorted by modern media:

And it's true we are immune/When fact is fiction and TV reality/And today the millions cry/We eat and drink while tomorrow they die.

Toward the end, the song takes a leap that was missed by some and misinterpreted by others:

The real battle just begun/To claim the victory Jesus won/On a Sunday, bloody Sunday[7]

The "real battle" and Jesus' victory were both references to peace. However, some took these words as a call to arms for the nationalist cause. To counter that, Bono always introduced the song by saying, "This is not a rebel song."[8] He wrapped himself in a white flag while performing it.

wanted Northern Ireland to remain part of the United Kingdom. The nationalists, who were Catholic, wanted Northern Ireland to join with the Republic of Ireland.

During the *October* tour, the situation in Northern Ireland had heated up. U2's nationality was suddenly an important part of the band's identity. Bono and his bandmates started to think deeply about what it meant to be Irish. Bono soon made it clear, however, that he would not take sides in the conflict. This son of a Protestant mother and a Catholic father was a peacemaker.

Edge began writing U2's hit song, "Sunday Bloody Sunday," and Bono finished it. The song is about a riot in Northern Ireland, on Sunday, January 30, 1972, that left 13 people dead. It makes a comparison to another "bloody Sunday," namely Jesus Christ's crucifixion, though Bono later admitted the idea probably went over most fans' heads. About the futility of war, it was, as Bono called it, a song of "hope and disgust."[9] It was the first time U2 had ever used a song to make a political statement. It signaled a new focus for the band, and for Bono. ◝

In 1997, mourners commemorate the twenty-fifth anniversary of Bloody
Sunday, an event also memorialized in U2's groundbreaking single.

Bono is carried by fans at a 1983 concert.

SUPERSTAR

In early 1983, "Sunday Bloody Sunday" came out on U2's next album, *War*. As signaled by the title, this watershed release addressed many of the world's political troubles, from the events in Northern Ireland to the weakening of communism in Eastern Europe. The album showcased a stark, stripped-down sound, against which Bono's emotional delivery was heightened. A success with both critics and fans, *War* outsold both of U2's previous albums combined.

Showman

Bono spent 1983 on the road. U2 started playing at stadiums with crowds of 20,000 or more. It was during this time that Bono earned his reputation as an extreme performer. Bono says:

> *I don't trust . . . a performer who's content on the stage, content with the distance between him or her and the audience. . . . I want to feel like the person on stage can stop playing a role, jump down, sit on my knee, follow me home. . . . I've always had that as a performer. I don't want people to feel comfortable in the relationship. I want to feel like it could snap.*[1]

On stage, Bono climbed on speakers. He jumped into the crowds. He left completely. In May, in Devore, California, Bono climbed scaffolding that supported lights for the stage. He went up 150 feet (46 m) or so. At the top, he planted an Irish flag and a white flag. The crowd went wild.

In June, at the Red Rocks Amphitheater in Denver, Colorado, U2 almost did not take the stage. The outdoor area had been deluged by rain all day, which stopped right before U2 went on. But the water was brushed off the stage, and the members took their places against the craggy backdrop. Lit by huge flame torches, the band looked ghostly in the evening mist. *Rolling Stone* later called the performance one of the 50 moments that changed rock and roll. Recordings from the evening became the basis for U2's very successful performance album and video, *Under a Blood Red Sky*.

Not Your Typical Eighties' Band

During the '80s, U2's political and spiritual message as well as its intense performances stood out at a time when much of the music industry was focused on superficial pop. As *Rolling Stone* said:

> At a time when rock music is dominated by swishy, style-soaked synthesizer bands whose main concern seems to be their ability to make people dance and forget the problems of the world, U2 stands out as a real exception. For one thing, they're a rock band in the more traditional sense of the word. Guitar, bass and drums—no electronic keyboards, no computerized drums. Granted, their sound is modern— dominated by Larry Mullen's boomy drumming and Dave "The Edge" Evans's droning, neopsychedelic guitar playing— but they're still a far cry from trendy technofunksters. . . . Then there are the band members themselves. Fashion-con- scious these guys are not. . . . Black jeans and a sleeveless black combat jacket will do just fine, thank you. And their lifestyle doesn't jibe with that of the usual rock & roller, either.[2]

Then, less than two weeks later, Bono went too far. At the Los Angeles Sports Stadium, Bono found himself trapped on a balcony 20 feet (6 m) high. What could he do? He jumped. Luckily, fans caught him. By the time he returned to stage, his clothes were in shreds from clawing fans, but he was unharmed.

Much to Bono's dismay, however, several fans followed his lead. People started throwing themselves off the balcony. Luckily, no one was seriously hurt. However, Bono's bandmates were livid with him—as he was with himself. After that experience, Bono changed as a performer. He said:

> *Somebody could have died at that concert, and it was a real sickener for me. It's meant a total revolution of what we are about live. We don't need to use a battering ram. It has to be down to the music.* [3]

THE UNFORGETTABLE FIRE

U2 was on the up-and-up. Other bands in their position might have cashed in, quickly putting out another album with more of the same. But that was not U2's style. Instead, Bono went on retreat in early 1984. He needed to reevaluate himself as an artist.

How could the band defy the public's expectations another time?

That summer, U2 recorded its next album at Slane Castle, located north of Dublin. The band recruited Brian Eno to produce the album. Eno, a musician in his own right, had worked with many successful artists, including David Bowie and the Talking Heads. U2 hoped Eno would help it move away from what was becoming a "U2 sound" and make its work more nuanced and sophisticated.

And Eno did encourage U2 to push its boundaries and experiment with new sounds. The result, *The Unforgettable Fire,* was a much warmer album than *War*. Though the topics were equally intense, the approach was more likely to inspire imagination than outrage. Bono's lyrics were richer, too, with more developed imagery.

"U2 have had two really rotten fashion phases. One was the *October* tour, where I had a skunk on my head. . . . The second was *The Unforgettable Fire* period. . . . And forget about bad-hair day, I was having bad-hair life. . . . I look at pictures from that period and I am the Prince of Mullet, and the only thing that's keeping that mullet away from pop history is a hat designed for a taller man. There's still people who can't like us because of that hair-do."[4]

—*Bono*

Uneasy Superstar

In 1985, *Rolling Stone* chose U2 as the Band of the Eighties. And 1985 was a dizzying year for Bono. He was almost constantly on tour. His enormous fame sometimes made it difficult for him to go out in public. People started treating him differently; he missed the natural encounters he used to have with fans. On top of that, for the first time in his life, he was extremely wealthy.

That July, U2 performed in Live Aid. Then, in September, Bono and Ali took their trip to Ethiopia. In 1986, he and Ali toured El Salvador to witness firsthand the effects of a U.S.-backed conflict in that Central American nation. Bono says:

> I may have been taking these trips to get away from being a pop star. In those far-off places people had no idea who I was and it felt great. . . . And, of course, in heightened fear and anxiety you are at your silliest. We would do the stupidest things, we'd behave like children. We had a lot of laughs.[5]

At the same time, Bono was deeply disturbed by what he saw. More and more, he found opportunities to use his fame and wealth for humanitarian purposes. One such opportunity was the Conspiracy of Hope tour to support the work

Bono and Sting address reporters at a 1986 news conference regarding the Conspiracy of Hope tour to raise awareness of human rights.

of the human-rights group Amnesty International. That successful project doubled Amnesty International's membership.

REFLECTIONS ON ART

Around this time, Bono was again evaluating himself as an artist, and he did not like what he saw. While he started writing for U2's next album, *The Joshua Tree,* he realized:

> . . . the lyrics on the first four albums are not really lyrics at all, they're sketches. I wasn't a writer really, I was a

painter, or an emoter or a shouter, I seemed to have almost a fear of writing; it was an advanced form of procrastination. I'd had it in my school work. You'd do anything but the thing you have to do because doing it brings judgment—fear of failure, probably. So just don't try. . . . I decided I'd better write some lyrics. I was reading more anyway, so I was more awake to the word. I discovered a love for writers and started to feel like one of them.[6]

Bono also took on an unresolved personal issue. He was feeling pulled in two directions between domestic life with Ali and the wandering life of the artist. To him, the question was: "Am I going to have kids and settle down and betray my gift or am I going to betray my marriage?"[7] Artists he admired most had not been able to resolve this question. For a time, he felt this tension would destroy him.

A Career or a Family?

Bono struggled with the question of whether he could balance a successful career with a happy family. Then he realized the creative importance of that tension:

"That tension, it turns out, is what makes me as an artist. Right in the centre of a contradiction, that's the place to be. There I was. Loyal [to Ali], but in my imagination filled with wanderlust, a heart to know God, a head to know the world, rock star who likes to run amok and sinner who knows he needs to repent."[8]

Then, he had a realization. Not only would
he accept the tension, he would embrace it. This
tension inspired the song "With or Without You."
The song was a standout on U2's most accomplished
album yet, *The Joshua Tree,* which would soon take U2
even higher into fame's stratosphere.

In the 1980s, Bono approached his growing fame with mixed feelings.

In 1988, U2 received its first Grammy award for The Joshua Tree.

STARTING OVER

Bono's travels and introspection culminated in *The Joshua Tree*, released in March 1987. Critics and fans alike were smitten.

The Joshua Tree was U2's first Number 1 album in the United States. It landed U2 its first Grammy awards, one of which was for Album of the Year. Its sales were unlike anything the band had ever seen. In April, U2 became only the third rock band in history (after the Beatles and the Who) to appear on the cover of *Time* magazine.

It seemed that U2—and especially Bono—was everywhere. Perhaps too much so. A backlash began against U2. Bono began to be perceived as pompous, verbose, and self-righteous. A joke started in the music industry: How many members of U2 does it take to change a lightbulb? Just one: Bono holds the lightbulb and the world revolves around him.

Even Bono seemed down on Bono. He appeared overwhelmed by the world's problems and the expectations of his fans.

RATTLE AND HUM

This downward spiral came to a head with U2's next project. Bono had always been a fan of the United States and American music. *Rattle and*

Political Songs

Bono's travels to Central America changed him forever. He was especially outraged about U.S. foreign policy in the area, which supported dictators. How could he translate his experiences into U2's music? In the recording studio, Bono hung up pictures and played videos of the horrors taking place in Central America. He described what he had seen and the stories he had heard to his bandmates. Afterward, he asked Edge, "Could you put that through your amplifier?"[1]

Two songs on *The Joshua Tree* directly address Central America. "Mothers of the Disappeared" is about those who had gone missing in El Salvador. "Bullet the Blue Sky" vehemently protested U.S. military involvement in the area.

Hum, a double-length album and movie, documents U2's trip across the nation during its *Joshua Tree* tour. The movie shows Bono meeting and playing music with such greats as Bob Dylan and B.B. King. The project's intention was to trace U2's journey through American culture and music.

Unfortunately, the final product did not turn out well. The film seemed unfocused, a mishmash of live footage that included what appeared to be a lot of speech making by Bono. Instead of coming across as fans of rock

---

Bono's Mentors

Though its message may not have come across properly, *Rattle and Hum* was intended as a praise to America's music giants. Bono says:

> I have a history of finding masters and making myself a student. Really my life has been that of an apprentice. That's why I'm a better writer this year than I was last year and I'll probably be a better writer next year. Everybody has a few things they've figured out and I will always be ready to humble myself in front of somebody who knows more than me.[2]

Bono says that one of the greatest rewards of fame has been that it has led him to the doorsteps of great musicians. Bono has worked with Frank Sinatra, Johnny Cash, Roy Orbison, and B.B. King, among others. During the mid-1980s, Bono saw a lot of Bob Dylan, his inspiration. Of Dylan, Bono says:

> He means more to me than anybody living in music or art. I don't see him as a songwriter, I see him as an artist. . . . I felt he saw something in me that wasn't fully formed. . . . The fact that we were selling ridiculous multi-platinum amounts of records wasn't what was important. I was growing, we were getting better, and that was what mattered.[3]

and roll, U2 seemed as if it was putting itself in the same class as the musical greats it meant to honor. As Edge put it, "Rather than using *The Joshua Tree* as a springboard to something even greater, we made a road movie and almost ran off the road."[4] Critics were scathing and fans were disappointed.

U2 experienced the worst failure of its career. What would its next move be? In characteristic fashion, the group decided to take time off to begin again. At a New Year's Eve party in Dublin in 1989, Bono told the crowd the band had run out of steam and was going to do something else for a while. As he later said:

> *The magic was gone, we couldn't see the stars. . . . And I realized that it was either over or else we'd have to go back to square one and dream it all up again.*[5]

BERLIN

When Bono turned 30 years old on May 10, 1990, it looked like he had everything going for him—a good marriage, fans eagerly awaiting his return, and more than enough money to last him a lifetime of luxury. Also, he now had a one-year-old daughter, Jordan, who had been born on his

Promotional material for Rattle and Hum, *what many considered a pretentious movie*

birthday the year before. But, creatively, Bono was
not satisfied. What would happen to U2?

As disastrous as *Rattle and Hum* was, Bono would
later say that the experience was necessary to U2's
development. It inspired U2 to reinvent itself.
Berlin, Germany, was a fitting location for U2 to
start over. Until November 1989, the city had been
literally divided by a concrete wall. On one side was
East Germany, controlled by the Soviet Union. On
the other side was West Germany. Now the two would

be one unified nation. Germany was starting over, and so was U2.

A Grueling Process

Though Bono is U2's lyricist, the band often composes together. Many songs develop in the recording studio. The band members both inspire and challenge each other. Bono has said that the process can be grueling. That was especially the case in Berlin. For the first time ever, the band was split by artistic differences. Bono and Edge wanted to explore something that had been considered off-limits to U2—the electronic sounds of dance music. They argued that only U2's exterior was changing. The music would still have substance.

Adam and Larry disagreed. Furthermore, Larry felt pushed out of the band, as drum machines would be taking over a significant portion of his contribution.

Bono has said that creative tension is a source of artistic power, and, in this case, the principle

Facing Limits

In Berlin, Bono found U2 needed more fixing than they had thought. He said, "What we thought were just hairline cracks that could be easily fixed turned out to be more serious, the walls needed underpinning, we had to put down new foundations or the house would fall down. In fact, it was falling down all around us. We were running up hotel bills and we had professional people, the U2 crew, staring at our averageness and scratching their heads. . . . We came face to face with our limitations as a group on a lot of levels."[6]

held true. Exhausted and on the verge of quitting, the band finally hit a groove with "One." The hauntingly beautiful number, appropriately, is about difference: "We're one, but we're not the same. We get to carry each other, carry each other . . . one."[7]

U2 spent the rest of the winter in Berlin recording its new album, what was to become *Achtung Baby.* After the album came out in November 1991, *Rolling Stone* declared it a successful comeback. In many ways, *Achtung Baby* took U2 back to its first album, *Boy.* As in that album, Bono's lyrics are deeply personal. Once again, he delves into the human heart.

In other ways, though, *Achtung Baby* was a huge departure for the band. Bono and Edge's vision had won out. U2 did away with simple beats for a new, distorted techno-sound. Bono also freely broke another U2 rule. For the first time ever, the new father (whose second child Memphis Eve was born in July) used the word *baby* in a U2 song. In fact, he did it 27 times throughout the album—not counting the title. The title itself is a line from a comedy film starring Mel Brooks, called *The Producers.* For the next several years, if Bono was going to sing about human frailty, he was going to do so with humor.

Bono and The Edge (shown in 2005) pushed for a new, electronic sound in the early 1990s.

Bono as "the Fly" performs in 1992.

RENEWAL

ono had a realization: "The best way to serve the age is to betray it."[1] For the next several years, U2 was going to do everything it was not supposed to. With the Zoo TV tour, U2 shows became over-the-top, multimedia extravaganzas.

Bono dove headfirst into the absurd—while never letting go of substance.

Zoo TV

The inspiration for Zoo TV came, in part, from media coverage of the first Gulf War. For the first time in history, people could watch war happening live. Like fireworks, exploding bombs aired in real time in living rooms around the globe. Viewers could channel surf from the war to children's programs to sitcoms to talk shows. On talk shows, ordinary people were revealing embarrassing and shocking details of their personal lives.

Bono wanted to create a U2 show that reflected and commented on this fragmentation of modern life. He wanted to challenge the audience, make them participate. He wanted to have fun while staying true to his quest for truth.

The scope of the Zoo TV tour was unprecedented: Each show required 52 trucks to carry 1,200 tons (1,089 tonnes) of equipment. The tour cost U2 $250,000 a day to operate.

"Zoo TV gets its energy from turning a stadium into a living room with TVs [and] with very personal songs on a huge PA. Metal guitars, dance grooves, trash art, something for all the family, something to annoy everyone. The more contradictions the better."[2]

—*Bono*

A Huge Risk

The Zoo TV tour was very costly. Though many companies would have eagerly helped foot the bill, U2 refused to accept a corporate sponsor. True to form, it did not want to be compromised in any way. The decision presented a huge risk. "If ten percent less people had come to see us, we'd have gone bankrupt," Bono says. "It was scary. . . . That's the only time I actually thought about failure."[4]

Everything was larger-than-life. Giant cars hung from cables over the audience. Enormous video screens flashed puzzling or outrageous words and phrases, such as "Art is manipulation" or "Rebellion is packaged."[3] Before the show, people had the opportunity to visit the Video Confessional, a leopard-skin telephone booth where they recorded their deepest secrets. During the show, bits of these confessions were projected on the TV screens.

Then there was Bono's performance style. He threw himself around stage. He dragged the mike stand like conquered prey. He went into spasms. Or he wrapped his arms around himself and sang with heartbreaking tenderness.

Bono also did pranks onstage. He called the White House so many times that he came to know the White House operators—though they never connected him to President George H.W. Bush. On one memorable night in Detroit, Bono called a local pizza parlor and ordered 10,000 pizzas. Once the stunned employees confirmed that the call was genuine, they managed to drive up with 100 pizzas within the hour. Bono passed out the pizzas to the audience and sent the delivery people home with $50 tips. Through such antics, Bono was showing the enormous and wide-ranging power of technology.

Bono's "Characters"

On stage, Bono no longer appeared as himself. He dressed up as one of several alter egos. Clad in tight black leather and dark sunglasses, the Fly was Bono's first invention.

Activist

In the summer of 1992, Bono was looking for a way to protest what he saw as a looming environmental crisis. Britain was planning to import nuclear waste in order to develop a nuclear processing plant at Sellafield, just across the Irish Sea. The environmental group Greenpeace warned that the new plant would dramatically increase radioactive pollution in and around the Irish Sea. What could the rock star do? First, U2 headlined at a gig to benefit the cause, pulling out all the Zoo-TV stops for a sold-out audience of more than 10,000. U2 reprogrammed the giant television screens for the occasion, so they flashed phrases such as "Contaminate," "Warhead," and "Nobody Is Promised a Tomorrow."

Early the next morning, U2 joined a group of Greenpeace activists in a bit of theatrical protest. The activists had been banned from staging a protest on government property surrounding the plant. So they found a way around it. Wearing full protective gear, the group arrived on a strip of beach offshore. They floated up to the strip in a line of inflated dinghies. Then Bono and the rest of the activists hauled heavy black barrels onto the sand. The barrels contain polluted soil from Ireland. The protestors put up giant signs with messages such as "Stop Sellafield" and "No Freedom of Speech Beyond This Point." Finally, they strung bright yellow and black hazard tape all over.

The Fly was a blowhard, a self-appointed expert on politics, love, and philosophy. Bono considered this obnoxious persona both a fool and a truth teller—the ultimate prankster.

Later Bono experimented with MirrorBall Man, an American televangelist type in a silver suit and a cowboy hat. Then there was Mr. MacPhisto, in white face paint and horns, the devil himself.

Who were these characters? Bono has said that each one is a comic exaggeration of aspects of his true personality. They were also Bono's response to the decadence and distortion of fame. For the first time ever, Bono was free to be the kind of rock star people accused him of being. Also, as Bono points out, the characters were like masks that allowed him greater freedom to express himself:

> *We couldn't be ourselves. All through the Eighties we tried to be ourselves and failed when the lights were on. Which is what set us up for Zoo TV. We decided to have some fun being other people, or at least other versions of ourselves. That's when we bumped into that great line of Oscar Wilde's: 'The mask reveals the man.' It's like people at a fancy dress party—they're free.*[5]

Dressed as Mr. MacPhisto, Bono places a call from stage during the Zoo TV tour.

PUSHING LIMITS

U2 was on a roll. During the tour, the band managed to put out another album, *Zooropa.* This work picked up where *Achtung Baby* left off. The theme of the album, Bono says, was about living with uncertainty and exploring boundaries. Bono's lyrics were even more crushingly personal, the sound even more experimental and futuristic. Before *Achtung Baby,* U2 had been wary of using electronic sounds and irony because the group saw them as soulless. Now it embraced both the new sound and the new approach head-on, discovering two more tools for finding meaning.

After *Zooropa,* U2's live performances became even more daring. During the early 1990s, war raged in the city of Sarajevo, in Bosnia. Media reports from Sarajevo were not accurately depicting the horrors of what was happening there. And, for the most part, the world was sitting idly by.

Bono desperately wanted to help. What could he do? U2 made a risky decision. It set up live satellite transmissions from Sarajevo. During the show, residents of the war-torn city would address the audience—live. The people of Sarajevo told the stunned crowds about rape, murders, looting, and other horrible atrocities. In one memorable instance, a girl said, "I wonder, what are you going to do for us in Sarajevo? I think the truth is you're not going to do anything."[6]

How could U2 continue with its show after that? At times, it seemed awkward or even in extremely bad taste. But U2 continued with the live feed. As Bono put it, "Live by satellite every night you had the extraordinary spectacle at a rock gig of reality trampling all over art."[7]

The war-torn city of Sarajevo was a great source of concern for Bono in the 1990s. He had a chance to see the destruction firsthand in 1995.

U2 arrives in Sarajevo in 1997, fulfilling its pledge to perform in the troubled city as soon as conditions allowed.

HUMANITARIAN

After the tour, Bono took some time to get "de-Zooed." He and Ali had barely seen each other during the past two years. In 1994, he reconnected with his family at a summerhouse in the south of France. He took on some side projects, which included cowriting a movie script, *The Million Dollar Hotel*.

PopMart

What would U2's next album be? How could the band surprise fans who were expecting surprise? In 1997, U2 released *Pop*. The experiment with technology was still on. Musically, *Pop* was, in many ways, the band's contribution to dance music— though several songs on the album were straight rock and roll. At the same time, the subject matter was all U2: God, faith, and grace.

Commercially, *Pop* was a huge success, but critics were not as taken with the work. And neither was the band. As Adam put it, "Whatever we were playing around with, it wasn't touching the right buttons."[1]

Soon U2 was on tour again. The PopMart tour was even more outrageous than Zoo TV, but the theme was different. If Zoo TV took on the media, PopMart took on commercialism. If Zoo TV's approach was ironic, PopMart's was fun and funky.

The band entered the stage from a giant, mirrored lemon. Other stage props were equally outrageous. A huge stuffed olive was skewered on a toothpick that was 100 feet (30.5 m) long.

McDonald's arches towered overhead. The tour also featured the largest video screen in the world.

Some fans, especially in the United States, did not get that U2 was mocking the superficiality of pop culture. Though PopMart was a huge commercial success, for the first time in years, U2 was not always performing to sold-out venues. Had U2 bitten off more than it could chew?

In September, the answer to that question came back a resounding "no." On September 23, the band played the concert of a lifetime in Sarajevo, Bosnia. U2 had wanted to play in the war-torn city during the Zoo TV tour, but conditions had been too dangerous. Now that the conflict was over, U2 had its chance.

"We wanted to make a party record but we came in at the end of the party. The dancing was over and there were a load of broken bottles and young people sleeping under tables and the odd [fight] in the garden between lovers who've [drunk] too much."[2]

—*Bono, describing* Pop

U2 would perform a full PopMart show, and as the trucks full of equipment rumbled down Bosnia's streets, people cheered. U2's arrival symbolized the true end of the war.

Fans from all around what was formerly Yugoslavia—people who had been at war just one year before— gathered for the event. Hundreds of North Atlantic Treaty Organization

Bono performs in front of the largest video screen in the world as part of a 1997 PopMart concert.

(NATO) peacekeeping officers in uniform also filled the stands. The pressure was on. But Bono was having trouble performing. His voice was shot from too much smoking and overuse. As Bono's voice faltered, the crowd of 45,000 filled in the gaps. They sang, hummed, and whistled when Bono could not. "It was one of the toughest and sweetest nights of my life," Bono said.[3]

A Historic Event

The PopMart tour ended in April 1998. But just one month later, Bono and U2 found themselves

performing at another history-making concert, this
time in Belfast, Northern Ireland.

On April 10, 1998, the Good Friday Peace
Agreement had been brokered to end the Troubles
in Northern Ireland. Bono believed the agreement
was a fair one and would bring lasting peace. A major
hurdle lay ahead, however. The agreement had to be
ratified in both Northern Ireland and Ireland. That
meant the general public—every citizen over 18—had
to vote on whether to approve it. In April, polls were
suggesting that it might not pass.

U2 agreed to perform a special benefit show in
support of the agreement. U2 was asked to share the
event with the two main leaders of each side—John
Hume, the leader of Northern Ireland's Catholic
minority, and David Trimble, the Protestant leader.
Bono said yes on one condition: The two leaders,
who had never even shaken hands, would appear on
stage together. The two men reluctantly agreed.

The night of the concert, on May 19, Bono
instructed the politicians not to say anything. Bono
stood between Hume and Trimble. He grabbed each
one by the arm and raised their hands in a salute.
It was an electrifying moment, played over and over
again in the media. Later, when the referendum

passed in both Northern Ireland and Ireland, many gave Bono and U2 credit for its success. Bono called the evening, "the greatest honor of my life."[4]

DIPLOMAT

The rest of the year found Bono struggling with tragedy. His father, Bobby Hewson, was diagnosed with cancer. And Bono was struggling with his own health problems: his voice was shot, and doctors had yet to rule out cancer. Without telling anyone, Bono went to the hospital for tests. For a short time, he thought he might have to give up everything. In the end, though, the problem was attributed to overuse of his voice, unhealthy habits, and allergies.

But there was good news, too. Ali was pregnant again. By the time their son Elijah was born in 1999, Bono was deeply involved in a new project. It was at this point in his life, around age 40, that Bono began a new role in his career as a humanitarian—respected diplomat.

The millennium was approaching and a new relief organization for Africa had formed around an ancient Biblical idea—the periodic forgiveness of debts. The millennium was the time, Jubilee 2000 argued, to cancel the debt owed by the world's poorest nations to the world's richest nations. For one, the debt was crushing Africa. The amount dwarfed aid coming in. Besides, Jubilee 2000 argued, the debt itself was unjust. Much of the money had been loaned to African dictators during the 1950s and 1960s. This was during the cold war between Western nations and the Soviet Union. The West wanted to keep communism at bay. The United States and other countries loaned money to African dictators simply because they were opposed to communism. These African leaders squandered the money, and now the next generation was being forced to pay.

Jubilee 2000 recruited Bono as the ideal spokesman. Bono was passionate about the cause. He was a gifted speaker. He also had the weight of celebrity to help him get access to world leaders.

Bono immersed himself in his new role. He read widely and spoke several times with scholars at Harvard University to understand the issues as deeply as he could. He wanted to be ready to meet with anyone and everyone who might help—or hinder— their progress.

Bono met with decision makers on both the left and the right. His role took him to meetings with

U.S. President Bill Clinton, Russian President Vladimir Putin, British Prime Minister Tony Blair, United Nations Secretary Kofi Annan, and even Pope John Paul II. With each one, he passionately pleaded Jubilee's case. He earned the reputation as an informed, articulate—and respected—statesman who appealed to each politician's humanity with both humility and wit.

And Bono's efforts paid off. Though Jubilee's work is still not over, several Western countries, including the United States, have dropped large amounts of debts—an act many had not thought possible.

BALANCE

What was happening with

"They Should Be Nervous"

When Bono meets with leaders, he goes in as himself, and sometimes, he says, people look at him strangely. But that does not bother him. In fact, when asked if he was ever nervous about his work, Bono had this to say:

When you've sold a lot of records, it's very easy to be megalomaniac enough to believe that you can change things. If you put your shoulder to the door, it might open. Especially if you're representing a greater authority than yourself. Call it love, call it justice, call it whatever you want. That's why I'm never nervous when I meet politicians. I think they should be nervous because I'm representing the poor and the wretched in this world. And I promise, history will be hard on this moment. And whatever thoughts you have about God, who He is or if He exists, most will agree that if there is a God, God has a special place for the poor. The poor are where God lives. So these politicians should be nervous, not me.[5]

On September 23, 1999, Bono had one of his most memorable meetings—with Pope John Paul II. The Catholic leader enthusiastically supported the work of Jubilee 2000, but the rock star and the pontiff connected on another level as well—humor. At one point, the pope gave Bono a set of rosary beads, for use in prayer. In return, Bono took off his dark, wraparound sunglasses and handed them to the pope. The smiling John Paul II put them on for a photo. Though the Vatican later destroyed the "unseemly" photo, Bono fondly remembered the moment. At a press conference, he referred to John Paul as "the first funky Pontiff."[7]

U2 during all this? The band was working on its next album, which would usher in yet another era for the group. Bono's hectic schedule undeniably delayed the album and caused frustration for the other band members. On the other hand, they deeply supported what he was doing. Also, Bono had always been a writer who worked in "bursts." His creative process meshed well with the new reality: he swept into town for short, intense recording sessions, while the rest of the band worked out the details.

And Bono has always been clear to his bandmates and the rest of the world that, no matter what, he will always be a musician first. In fact, he believes his gift as a musician feeds his other work. As he puts it:

> My gift is that I'm a singer, a songwriter and a performer. I just happened to have learned other skills to protect that gift, and those skills seem to suit political activism.[6]

*In 2002, Bono met with President George W. Bush
to discuss third-world debt.*

Bono takes in the view from his Boston hotel room in December 2005, shortly after he was named a "Person of the Year" by Time *magazine.*

An Unusual "Man of Peace"

n October 2000, U2 ended an era. Its next album, *All That You Can't Leave Behind*, signaled the end of U2's experiment with dance music. This album featured U2's classic stripped-down guitar, drums, and bass. At the same time, the composition was richer than the band's 1980s work. The work also had the feel of a celebration, shown best by the hit "Beautiful Day." *All That You Can't Leave Behind* was deemed a masterpiece by fans and critics alike.

A LIFE-CHANGING YEAR

For Bono and the United States as well, 2001 was full of life-changing events. In May, Bono's fourth child, John Abraham, was born. At the same time, Bono's father was dying of cancer. Bono flew home from gigs as often as possible to sit by his father's bedside. Though the two had shared many struggles, Bono says of his father, "I felt close to him towards the end."[1]

Bobby Hewson died that August, and Bono and his brother buried their father themselves. Bono did not cancel any concerts. In fact, he played in London the very night his father died. He compared performing to

"Bono was always larger than life. . . . He is also extremely complex. You don't know what's going on in that head of his and you might not want to. He has an explosive, unpredictable side to him. He's got an insatiable appetite for adventure and he will do almost anything and go anywhere to satisfy that. Being as successful as he is has real downsides, the opportunities afforded him are mind-blowing, the responsibility that comes with it is immense. It is extraordinary how he can survive and thrive on it. His faith is his anchor and I think that's what enables him to navigate his way through and come out relatively unscathed."[2]

—*U2 drummer Larry Mullen*

the Irish tradition of "keening," or wailing loudly, at a funeral:

> *I guess I did my grieving for my father keening in front of twenty thousand people singing U2 songs. They really carried me, those songs and my three mates. After the shows I felt much better.* [3]

The very next month—after September 11, 2001—Bono's performances would offer healing in a similar way. This time the grieving was the American public. It was shocked and saddened by the terrorist attacks on the World Trade Center towers and the Pentagon that left thousands dead and a nation forever changed.

U2's soulful, haunting music touched the public in a profound way. During concerts, "there was anger, rage, patriotism, sadness, everything became frighteningly extreme," Larry Mullen said. [4] At one point, U2 started rolling the names of the 9/11 victims on screens while they sang "One." Was that too much? Adam was not sure, but Bono was. Adam later noted that Bono's decision allowed the group to hit a nerve with people while opening their minds at the same time.

THE FIGHT FOR AFRICA

Bono's career was flourishing, but, once again, he was not satisfied. Africa haunted him. In March 2002, Bono officially kicked off a new organization. Named DATA, it stood for Debt, AIDS, Trade, Africa. DATA pushed Western governments for aid, new trade laws, and affordable AIDS drugs; it also pushed African governments toward democracy. Bono lobbied every influential person he could gain access to in Washington to spread his urgent message: Africa was gripped in a poverty and health crisis.

Bono's Approach

Bono has a history of rubbing elbows with those who hold starkly different views from his. One such person was Senator Jesse Helms, whose controversial beliefs included one that Satan lured young people to drugs and violence through pop music. Nonetheless Bono and Helms connected over the issue of Africa—leaving Helms in tears.

What makes Bono so persuasive? For one, Bono comes prepared. His deep understanding of the issues has impressed even the most suspicious politician. In 2001, Treasury Secretary Paul O'Neill initially refused to meet Bono. But after their session went three times longer than it was supposed to, O'Neill came around. Of Bono, he said, "He's a serious person. He cares deeply about these issues, and you know what? He knows a lot about them."[5]

Bono also tailors his approach depending on whom he's meeting. For example, he has swayed Republicans who are opposed to foreign aid in principle by appealing to them as Christians. (One of the many facts he cites is how many times the Bible addresses caring for the poor—2,103.)

In addition to facts and celebrity power, his arsenal includes wit, humor, theatrics, and, most of all, his own passion.

*At an HIV clinic in South Africa, Bono plays
with 11-month-old Thomas Gqubile.*

In addition to DATA, Bono and Bobby Shriver,
a music industry executive, cofounded (RED). As its
Web site stresses, (RED) is not a charity, not a cause,
and not a theory. It teams up with giant corporations
such as Apple, Gap, and Starbucks to sell special
(RED) products and services. A portion of those
profits goes to fight AIDS in Africa.

In 2005, Bono also helped Ali create a line of clothing called EDUN (which is "nude" backward). The casual and affordable clothes are made in developing areas of the world, especially Africa, and use organic fabrics. In 2008, DATA became incorporated into Bono's One campaign, which, with more than 2 million members, uses grassroots methods to lobby governments and raise awareness of extreme poverty, particularly in Africa.

Through all these efforts, Bono has seen incredible results. One of his biggest successes was convincing President George W. Bush, in 2002, to commit $15 billion to fight AIDS in Africa. Also, (RED) generated more than $120 million in its first two years. At the same time, Bono has seen his share of heartache and frustration. Today, what Bono calls "stupid" poverty is still overwhelming. For example, more than 1 billion people on Earth do not have access to clean drinking water. In 2007, 881,000 people died of malaria—a disease that can be treated with a $2 dose of medication. Bono's work is far from over.

Bono has received many awards for his work already, though. In 2005, he was *Time* magazine's Person of the Year (along with Bill and Melinda

Gates). Bono has also been nominated for (but has not won) a Nobel Peace Prize. However, in 2008, he was awarded the Nobel "Man of Peace" Prize, a prestigious award given by Nobel Peace Prize winners.

STILL A ROCK STAR

Bono is a man of peace, but the media also occasionally casts him as a stereotypical rock star. Bono is still the prankster from Lypton Village and the chameleon from Zoo TV. Three years before he won the *Time* magazine award, he drew sharp criticism for another act: he flew a hat first-class from London to Italy to wear for a performance. "The right to be ridiculous is something I hold dear," he has said, and he freely exercises that right.[6]

Bono's time in the recording studio has certainly gone down, but, he says, he is always writing. In 2004, the band released *How to Dismantle an Atomic Bomb,* a raw, guitar-driven, record that sold faster than any other U2 album to date. In early 2009, the band released *No Line on the Horizon* and began promoting another performance tour.

And while Bono has been lauded by humanitarian groups, U2 has been gathering its own share of awards. In 2005, the group was inducted into the Rock and Roll Hall of Fame. Then, in 2006, it swept the Grammies with five awards, including Album of the Year.

Bono lives his life at an almost unimaginably fast pace: he goes from meeting to party to rally to phone call to performance, and he travels more often than he is at home. Some of that travel is to the poorest nations on Earth. Because he never wants his work to become an abstraction, he insists on seeing firsthand the devastating effects of poverty and human indifference.

Bono has explained how he is able to still sustain his faith:

The reason [my faith] can survive any awfulness the world can throw at it, is that I am not surprised by evil. To me, we live in a jungle and I'm expecting at any moment that something will try and eat me. . . . I'm more surprised when

"There are moments when you hear the voice crack and you think: This has gone too far. I should be treating my voice with a bit more care. But most of the time I would come back from those marches, rallies, meetings or conference rooms and arrive on the stage two feet taller. I'm floating because of what could come out of all of this. And I feel God's blessing in it. You can't out-give God, I've noticed. I feel like I've been carried by people's prayers. And it hasn't hurt me at all. I'm in top shape. The gigs were brilliant. My voice has never been as strong. How could that be? It's crazy."[7]

—Bono, on balancing his activist work with his work as a performer

the punch isn't thrown. But that does not make me cynical. In fact, rather the opposite. I'm amazed at people's ability to sacrifice for each other. I'm amazed at how people can show love where it's not expected and how love can conjoin disparate groups. I'm just amazed at human beings.[8] —

U2 performs at the inauguration of President Barack Obama in 2009.

TIMELINE

1960	1974	1976
On May 10, Bono is born in Dublin, Ireland.	Bono's mother, Iris Hewson, dies on September 10.	In September, the future members of U2 meet to start a band.

1985	1987	1989
In July, U2 plays in Live Aid; Bono takes his first trip to Africa.	U2 releases *The Joshua Tree* to wide acclaim in March.	Bono's first of four children, his daughter Jordan, is born on May 10.

1980	1982	1983
U2 releases its first full-length album, *Boy*, in October.	Bono marries Ali Stewart on August 21.	U2 releases *War*, its first album to address political themes.

1991	1992	1997
U2 releases *Achtung Baby*, introducing a new synthesized sound.	The Zoo TV tour begins.	U2 releases *Pop*, its tribute to dance music; PopMart begins in April.

TIMELINE

1997	**1998**	**1998**
In September, U2 plays in the war-torn city of Sarajevo.	In May, U2 plays a historic concert on behalf of the Good Friday Peace Agreement in Belfast.	Bono begins as a spokesman for the Jubilee 2000 campaign.

2004	**2005**	**2005**
How to Dismantle an Atomic Bomb becomes U2's fastest-selling album.	U2 is inducted into the Rock and Roll Hall of Fame in March.	Bono is named *Time's* Person of the Year.

2000	2001	2002
In October, U2 releases *All That You Can't Leave Behind*, going back to a stripped-down sound.	Bono's father, Bob Hewson, dies.	In March, DATA officially begins; Bono meets with President George W. Bush.

2006	2008	2009
Bono's (RED) campaign kicks off.	Bono is awarded the Nobel "Man of Peace" Prize.	U2 releases *No Line on the Horizon*.

Essential Facts

Date of Birth
May 10, 1960

Place of Birth
Dublin, Ireland

Parents
Bobby and Iris Hewson

Education
Mount Temple High School, Dublin

Marriage
Alison Stewart (August 21, 1982)

Children
Jordan, Memphis Eve, Elijah, John Abraham

Career Highlights
Bono is the lead singer and songwriter of U2, one of the most famous rock and roll bands of all time. For more than 30 years, he has led the band through many different sounds. Through it all, U2 has remained a band with a message—ready to take on political themes as well as mine the human heart.

Societal Contributions

Bono is also known as an activist, especially in the cause of extreme poverty. In 1998, he became the spokesman for Jubilee 2000, an organization working to eliminate third world debt. In this role, Bono met with U.S. President Bill Clinton and other world leaders. In 2002, he expanded his work for Africa by launching DATA (Debt, AIDS, Trade, Africa) with Bobby Shriver. Bono has also been instrumental in the (RED) and One campaigns.

Conflicts

As a lyricist, Bono thinks deeply about the problems of his times as well as the frailty of the human heart. He also has an adrenaline-driven personality, which drives him to extremes. These character traits, compounded by the death of his mother, made Bono an angry and violent teenager. Bono is also a risk-taker, which has led him into scrapes and projects he later regretted. However, this same character trait has also undoubtedly created his success as a rock star and humanitarian.

Quote

"I'm a scribbling, cigar-smoking, wine-drinking, Bible-reading band man. A show-off . . . who loves to paint pictures of what I can't see. A husband, father, friend of the poor and sometimes the rich. An activist traveling salesman of ideas. Chess player, part-time rock star, opera singer, in the loudest folk group in the world."—*Bono*

Additional Resources

Select Bibliography

Assayas, Michka. *Bono in Conversation with Michka Assayas*. New York: Riverhead Books, 2005.

The Editors of Rolling Stone. *U2: The Ultimate Compendium of Interviews, Articles, Facts and Opinions from the Files of Rolling Stone*. New York: Rolling Stone Press, 1994.

Jackson, Laura. *Bono: His Life, Music, and Passions*. New York: Citadel Press, 2001.

U2. *U2 by U2*. New York: HarperCollins, 2006.

Wall, Mick. *Bono: In the Name of Love*. New York: Thunder's Mouth Press, 2005.

Wenner, Jann S., and Joe Levy, Eds. *The Rolling Stone Interviews*. New York: Back Bay Books, 2007.

Further Reading

Ditchfield, Christin. *Bono*. Ann Arbor, MI: Cherry Lake Publishing, 2008.

McIntosh, Kenneth. *U2*. Broomall, PA: Mason Crest Publishers, 2008.

Schaffer, David. *Bono*. Farmington Hills, MI: Lucent Books, 2004.

Web Links

To learn more about Bono, visit ABDO Publishing Company online at **www.abdopublishing.com**. Web sites about Bono are featured on our Book Links page. These links are routinely monitored and updated to provide the most current information available.

Places to Visit

The Rock and Roll Hall of Fame and Museum
1100 Rock and Roll Boulevard, Cleveland, OH 44114
216-781-ROCK (7625)
www.rockhall.com
Celebrate and learn about rock and roll music. Pay tribute to Bono and other musical legends.

The United Nations
1st Ave & 46th St., New York, NY 10017
212-963-TOUR (8687)
www.un.org
Take a guided tour of the world's peacekeeping body. Learn about human rights, poverty, and other global issues that Bono cares about.

A U2 Concert
Go to www.U2.com to find out when and where U2 will be playing live.

GLOSSARY

activist
A person who campaigns for social and political change.

alter ego
A person's less prominent personality.

amateur
A person who pursues music, art, or some other skill as a hobby.

cold war
A period after World War II marked by intense bad feeling (though never actual war) between communist countries, led by the Soviet Union, and noncommunist countries, led by the United States.

commercialism
Society's emphasis on money and things at the expense of people.

crisis of faith
A time in a person's life when he or she despairs about the meaningfulness of life itself.

decadence
Extremely self-indulgent behavior.

disco
Dance music that was popular in the 1970s.

extravaganza
An over-the-top event.

Grammy
A prestigious award given annually in the United States to people in the recording business.

grueling
Difficult and exhausting.

humanitarian
A person who cares deeply about and tries to improve other people's lives.

improvise
> To create while performing.

introspection
> The practice of thinking deeply about one's life.

ironic
> Causing amusement by happening in the opposite way of what is expected.

lyricist
> Someone who writes the words to songs.

mentor
> An experienced person who helps others in his or her field.

millennium
> The point in time at which a period of 1,000 years ends, most recently the year 2000.

pontiff
> Another word for pope; the head of the Roman Catholic Church.

punk rock
> A rock movement in the 1970s characterized by a loud, brash sound rather than musicality.

superficiality
> A lack of depth of character or human understanding.

televangelist
> A preacher with a TV show; televangelists have a reputation of asking viewers to send money.

zealous
> Extremely eager about a cause or a belief.

Source Notes

Chapter 1. Leaps of Faith
1. U2. *U2 by U2*. New York: HarperCollins, 2006. 345.
2. Michka Assayas. *Bono in Conversation with Michka Assayas*. New York: Riverhead Books, 2005. 210.
3. U2. *U2 by U2*. New York: HarperCollins, 2006. 164.
4. Mick Wall. *Bono: In the Name of Love*. New York: Thunder's Mouth Press, 2005. 8.
5. David Schaffer. *Bono*. Farmington Hills, MI: Lucent Books, 2004. 51–52.
6. Josh Tyrangiel and Benjamin Nugent. "Bono." *Time*. 4 Mar. 2002. 7 May 2009 <http://www.time.com/time/magazine/article/0,9171,1001931-1,00.html>.
7. Michka Assayas. *Bono in Conversation with Michka Assayas*. New York: Riverhead Books, 2005. 81.
8. Ibid. 10.
9. U2. *U2 by U2*. New York: HarperCollins, 2006. 314.
10. Michka Assayas. *Bono in Conversation with Michka Assayas*. New York: Riverhead Books, 2005. 43.
11. Mick Wall. *Bono: In the Name of Love*. New York: Thunder's Mouth Press, 2005. 15–16.

Chapter 2. Dublin Childhood
1. U2. *U2 by U2*. New York: HarperCollins, 2006. 15.
2. Mick Wall. *Bono: In the Name of Love*. New York: Thunder's Mouth Press, 2005. 23.
3. U2. *U2 by U2*. New York: HarperCollins, 2006. 15.
4. Michka Assayas. *Bono in Conversation with Michka Assayas*. New York: Riverhead Books, 2005. 16.
5. Ibid. 9.
6. U2. *U2 by U2*. New York: HarperCollins, 2006. 161.
7. Ibid. 16.

Chapter 3. Troubled Teen
1. Michka Assayas. *Bono in Conversation with Michka Assayas*. New York: Riverhead Books, 2005. 12.
2. Ibid. 13.
3. U2. *U2 by U2*. New York: HarperCollins, 2006. 20.
4. Kenneth McIntosh. *U2*. Broomall, PA: Mason Crest Publishers,

2008. 16.
5. "Band on the Run." <i>Time.</i> 27 Apr. 1987. 8 Sep. 2005.
8 May 2009 <http://www.time.com/time/magazine/
article/0,9171,964182,00.html>.
6. Mick Wall. <i>Bono: In the Name of Love.</i> New York: Thunder's Mouth
Press, 2005. 45.
7. Ibid. 38.
8. Ibid. 40.

Chapter 4. Rise to Fame
1. Michka Assayas. <i>Bono in Conversation with Michka Assayas.</i> New York:
Riverhead Books, 2005. 53.
2. Mick Wall. <i>Bono: In the Name of Love.</i> New York: Thunder's Mouth
Press, 2005. 70.
3. Ibid. 76.
4. The Editors of Rolling Stone. <i>U2: The Ultimate Compendium of
Interviews, Articles, Facts and Opinions from the Files of Rolling Stone.</i> New York:
Rolling Stone Press, 1994. 1.
5. U2. <i>U2 by U2.</i> New York: HarperCollins, 2006. 101.
6. The Editors of Rolling Stone. <i>U2: The Ultimate Compendium of
Interviews, Articles, Facts and Opinions from the Files of Rolling Stone.</i> New York:
Rolling Stone Press, 1994. 1.

Chapter 5. Rock Star
1. U2. <i>U2 by U2.</i> New York: HarperCollins, 2006. 180.
2. Michka Assayas. <i>Bono in Conversation with Michka Assayas.</i> New York:
Riverhead Books, 2005. 313.
3. Ibid. 51.
4. U2. <i>U2 by U2.</i> New York: HarperCollins, 2006. 190.
5. U2. "Gloria." U2.com. 2009. 8 May 2009 <http://www.
u2.com/discography/lyrics/lyric/song/50/>.
6. U2. <i>U2 by U2.</i> New York: HarperCollins, 2006. 130.
7. U2. "Sunday Bloody Sunday." U2.com. 2009. 8 May 2009
<http://www.u2.com/discography/lyrics/lyric/song/127>.
8. Mick Wall. <i>Bono: In the Name of Love.</i> New York: Thunder's Mouth
Press, 2005. 98.
9. Laura Jackson. <i>Bono: His Life, Music, and Passions.</i> New York: Citadel
Press, 2001. 44.

Source Notes Continued

Chapter 6. Superstar
1. Michka Assayas. *Bono in Conversation with Michka Assayas*. New York: Riverhead Books, 2005. 211.
2. The Editors of Rolling Stone. *U2: The Ultimate Compendium of Interviews, Articles, Facts and Opinions from the Files of Rolling Stone*. New York: Rolling Stone Press, 1994. 9.
3. Ibid. 17.
4. U2. *U2 by U2*. New York: HarperCollins, 2006. 161.
5. Ibid. 177.
6. Ibid. 179.
7. Ibid. 181.
8. Ibid.

Chapter 7. Starting Over
1. U2. *U2 by U2*. New York: HarperCollins, 2006. 179.
2. Ibid. 196.
3. Ibid. 199.
4. Ibid. 207.
5. Ibid. 213.
6. Ibid. 225.
7. U2. "One." U2.com. 2009. 8 May 2009 <http://www.u2.com/ discography/lyrics/lyric/song/97/>.

Chapter 8. Renewal
1. U2. *U2 by U2*. New York: HarperCollins, 2006. 225.
2. Mick Wall. *Bono: In the Name of Love*. New York: Thunder's Mouth Press, 2005. 179–180.
3. Jann S. Wenner and Joe Levy, Eds. *The Rolling Stone Interviews*. New York: Back Bay Books, 2007. 211.
4. Michka Assayas. *Bono in Conversation with Michka Assayas*. New York: Riverhead Books, 2005. 37–38.
5. U2. *U2 by U2*. New York: HarperCollins, 2006. 235.
6. Jann S. Wenner and Joe Levy, Eds. *The Rolling Stone Interviews*. New York: Back Bay Books, 2007. 210.
7. U2. *U2 by U2*. New York: HarperCollins, 2006. 253.

Chapter 9. Humanitarian

1. Laura Jackson. *Bono: His Life, Music, and Passions*. New York: Citadel Press, 2001. 159.

2. U2. *U2 by U2*. New York: HarperCollins, 2006. 269.

3. Laura Jackson. *Bono: His Life, Music, and Passions*. New York: Citadel Press, 2001. 163.

4. Michka Assayas. *Bono in Conversation with Michka Assayas*. New York: Riverhead Books, 2005. 173.

5. Ibid. 123.

6. U2. *U2 by U2*. New York: HarperCollins, 2006. 344.

7. Laura Jackson. *Bono: His Life, Music, and Passions*. New York: Citadel Press, 2001. 190.

Chapter 10. An Unusual "Man of Peace"

1. U2. *U2 by U2*. New York: HarperCollins, 2006. 307.

2. Ibid. 344.

3. Mick Wall. *Bono: In the Name of Love*. New York: Thunder's Mouth Press, 2005. 282.

4. Josh Tyrangiel and Benjamin Nugent. "Bono." *Time*. 4 Mar. 2002. 7 May 2009 <http://www.time.com/time/magazine/article/0,9171,1001931-1,00.html>.

5. Ibid.

6. Ibid.

7. U2. *U2 by U2*. New York: HarperCollins, 2006. 339.

8. Ibid. 300.

INDEX

ABOUT THE AUTHORS

Thom Winckelmann is a freelance editor, writer, and writing consultant living in Central Florida, where he also teaches college-level history and humanities. Currently at work on his doctoral dissertation toward a PhD in history, he specializes in Holocaust and genocide studies.

Lynn Abushanab is a children's book writer and editor in Minneapolis, Minnesota.

PHOTO CREDITS

Charles Dharapak/AP Images, cover; Joe Schaber/AP Images, 6; Ron Frehm/AP Images, 10; Seth Wenig/AP Images, 15; James A. Sugar/National Geographic/Getty Images, 16; Chris Bacon/AP Images, 23; Alvara Barrientos/AP Images, 24; Kevork Djansezian/AP Images, 27; Martyn Goddard/Corbis, 33; David Corio/Getty Images, 34; Neal Preston/Corbis, 41; Wally Fong/AP Images, 42; Axel Seidemann/AP Images, 46; Paul McErlane/AP Images, 49; Joe Giron/Corbis, 50; Bill Kostroun/AP Images, 56; Jon Sievert/Getty Images, 59; Mark Lennihan/AP Images, 60; Paramount Pictures/Photofest, 64; Denis Poroy/AP Images, 67; Wildredo Lee/AP Images, 68; Andrew Murray/Sygma/Corbis, 73; Santiago Lyon/AP Images, 75; Sava Radovanovic/AP Images, 76; Lennox McLendon/AP Images, 79; Ron Edmonds/AP Images, 85; Antonin Kratochvil/AP Images, 86; Juda Ngwenya/AP Images, 90; Alex Brandon/AP Images, 95